I AM

ARCANA

A POETRY COLLECTION BY

KRISTY NICOLLE

First published by Kristy Nicolle, United Kingdom, December 2021

(1ˢᵗ EDITION)
Published December 2021 by Kristy
Nicolle
Copyright © 2021 Kristy Nicolle
Edited By- Jaimie Cordall

Poetry Collection

Disclaimer:
This e-book is written in U.K English by personal preference of the author. This is a work of fiction. Names, characters, businesses, places, events and incidents are either the products of the author's imagination or used in a fictitious manner. Any resemblance to actual persons, living or dead, or events is purely coincidental.

ISBN: 978-1-911395-23-2

www.kristynicolle.com

CONTENTS

For the women who practice unapologetically.
Thank you.

Without you I would never have known
I was a witch in denial,
or a poet in hiding.

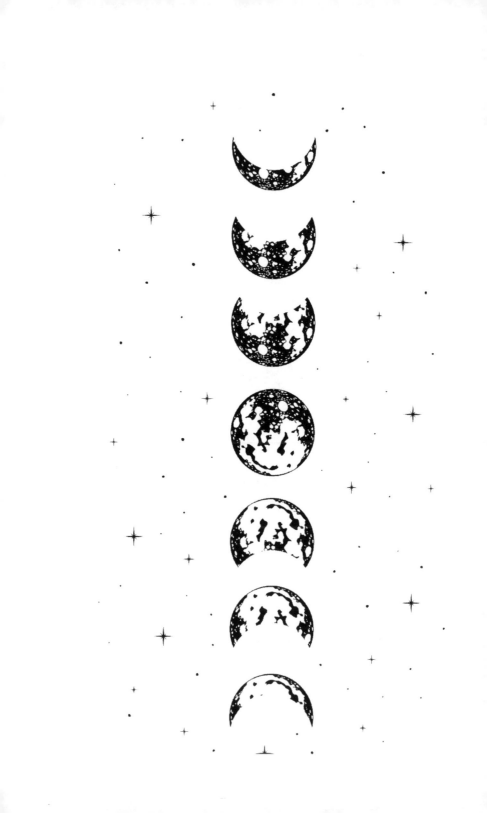

THE
FOOL

NEW BEGINNINGS /INNOCENCE/ SPONTANEITY

THE FOOL

i

He would compare thee to a summer's day...

Can he not see the thunder,
rolling
behind your lips?

Or the lightning,
forking
within your eyes?

being underestimated
simplified
because of your
femininity

2

THE FOOL

ii

I pity the fool
who underestimates me...

Though,
not as much,
as I pity the fool
who underestimates herself.

THE FOOL

iii

I see you,
staring.

At the blank page.
The unmoulded clay.
The alabaster canvas.

I know the taunts,
bringing fears into startling,
vivid life.

Begin

I whisper...
Breath catching with excitement.

Quivering,
you pick up the pen,
the brush,
the clay.

Begin

I urge.
No time to waste.
Your future awaits.

There is fire in your potential,

4

And magic in the future failures from which you
will rise.

Be the fool you are.
And simply
Begin

comfort in
failure,
in sweet
foolishness.

Expression do far:
Approachable poetry,
self-discovery,
self reflection

5

THE
MAGICIAN

INNOVATIVE/ INITIATIVE/ FOCUS

THE MAGICIAN

i

And just like that,
She knew.

Raw, she was magic.
And magic was enough.

THE MAGICIAN

ii

Her magic was not
turning water into wine.

But rather morphing
her frown
into a heart-shattering smile

and her tears
into laughter soul deep.

explorations of femininity

THE MAGICIAN

cosmic

iii

The fool I was.

The magician I am

transitions,
discovery

The High Priestess I hope to become.

Ever drawing worlds,
suns, moons,
and stars,
from the deck of this life.

They speak for what lies within.
tell the stories of my universe,
giving voice to the stardust in my veins,
bringing my intuition to life.

The Cards Know all,
because,
and only because,
I am Arcana.

She knows all
the cards are a fool
to undig things
She already Knows
deep down .

9

THE
HIGH PRIESTESS

CREATIVITY/ INTUITION/ WISDOM

HIGH PRIESTESS

i

Sage on her fingertips,
flowers in her hair,
the goddess in me is stirring
there's magic in the air.

Feet beat the earth,
Dancing around the flames,
this wild woman within me
is not one to be tamed.

They look,
they fear,
they do not understand.
A high priestess is rising,
and it's one they can't command.

11

HIGH PRIESTESS

ii

When I saw you
I knew.

Call it intuition,
Call it the universe
Screaming,
A war cry just for me.

Your twin flame
reached out across time
burnt the world I knew to cinders

When I saw you
I knew.

That in you
I had found the woman,
who would help me
rise again from the ash.

Only this time
as myself.

HIGH PRIESTESS

iii

No matter how
her eyes may fall,
her spine wilt,
her voice fade,
she is never really gone

inner strength,
rebirth

Only waiting.

For that first spring day,
the odd kind word,
that soft half smile,
that one who sees
what she has forever been.

To bloom again,
vivaciously vivid,
for those who admire,
that once trampled by heavy feet.

THE
EMPRESS

ABUNDANCE/BEAUTY/FERTILITY

THE EMPRESS

I

Lashes flutter, wild.
Lips tremble, a silent shockwave.
Flawless alabaster swells with new heat.

Twin peaks tremor atop tectonic ribs,
that rise and fall,
cradling this, the epicentre.
Too late to sound the sirens now.

My heart beneath this cage does quake,
For you, my lust, a wanton ache.

THE EMPRESS

ii

She is beautiful.
Not of pale skin,
full breasts,
and lustrous hair,
nor high heels and
painted lips.

She is beautiful
because this uneven skin tone
is her own.
Just like that frizzy mane,
and her curvaceous disproportion
of ample hips and petite chest.

She wears nothing but a gentle knowing smile,
which fits her like a glove.
Stunning simply because she walks barefoot
through wildflowers,
at home with the earth,
from which she came,
entirely.

THE EMPRESS

iii

I do not swell with child,
but a thousand festering words.

Like angry bees,
they kick and swarm
within my core,
at home for far too long.

Ink breaks like waters,
and the labour begins.

Hand cramping,
I hunch over the page,
birthing those words,
despite the pain.

Toiling 'til the hour of dawn,
when with an exhausted cry,
at last,
I am free.

At least until tomorrow.

THE
EMPEROR

AUTHORITY/ LEADERSHIP/ CONTROL

THE EMPEROR

i

He painted her skin
bloody red
ghostly white
and deep bruised blue.

Then he called it love.

THE EMPEROR

ii

Why must they wrap
these fertile vines
in chains?

Yet not permit us to prune the roses?

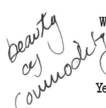

Why must we bloom for them,
whether painful,
or fatal?

Yet none help tend the buds.

For their seed
is deemed
unstoppable.

Yet their flowers yesterday's news.

Shredded in our laps,
such precious petals,
heavy and forgotten
ours alone to repair.

Yet we planted them together.

Don't you remember?

THE EMPEROR

iii

He was a mountain
majestic and fierce
indomitable against the sky
inspiring all around him to climb.

Yet she was a slag pile,
blocking the sunrise,
inconvenient in every way,
a monolith to their shortcomings.

Same picture
different View.

THE
HIEROPHANT

FORGIVENESS/ TEACHERS/ TRADITIONS

THE HIEROPHANT

i

Forgive.

Not for them,
but for you,
dear child.

Life is hard enough,
without carrying rage
toward someone,
not worth the air in your lungs,
nor one moment of
the precious time you have left.

learning to forgive

THE HIEROPHANT

II

Honey drips,
from fingertips.

Sage smoke
smudges the air.

She calls on them,
wise women condemned,
to aid her,
now their heir.

She sweeps the floor,
from left to right,
clearing the negative
from this night,
and stares into a flickering flame,
clutching the hilt of her athame.

The spell it forms upon her lips,
her blade through flesh,
like butter slips.

Red blood then falls,
upon the floor,
this girl, a witch,
forever more.

THE HIEROPHANT

iii

My mother's gifts,
weren't made of gold,
but tincture herbs,
and stories old.

Her love for me,
shown not with gifts,
but knowledge of the tides
and drifts.

Her spirit is with me,
even now,
in nature's wild
and solemn vow.

Her words this day,
stay with me still,
Harm Ye None
Do As Ye Will.

THE
LOVERS

LOVE/ UNION/ HARMONY

THE LOVERS

i

You marked me with no scars,
but one thousand simple acts.

A million gentle traces,
and curves of endless care.

love

Step back and see my strength

A mandala of devotion.

A work of your design.

THE LOVERS

ii

The kiss burns,
a scorching, eternal rage.
Encased by the salted twin falls
of bitter pearly tears.

They sizzle against my lips,
turning the taste of you charred,
[as you take what you want
  and give nothing back]

one jaded

THE LOVERS

iii

It was not only your precious words
that moved me so.
But how your breath carried them,
as if a single shudder
would rattle their steel truth to dust.

3 poems per card! each with a particular theme or interpretation of the card

THE
CHARIOT

PASSION/ WILLPOWER/ AMBITION

THE CHARIOT

i

The lashing bites,
a tongue of razors
carving my flesh and blood,
into a map
of my suffering.

I turn,
looking back,
wondering who
would torture me so.

Only to find
the one
holding the whip
is me.

THE CHARIOT

ii

My chariot,
dragged by will and faith,
hands raw on the reins,
shall ride ever higher
so I might caress the stars.

THE CHARIOT

iii

Catalogue of a person rediscovering themselves

Driving hunger,
endless pain,
sleepless nights,
rest in vain.

rhyme scheme

Sweat of brow,
grunts too strained,
tears of effort,
for things ingrained.

Are you happy?
Are you well?
A road of passionless toil
leads only to hell.

Stop the wheels,
put on the brake,
slower won't kill you
for heaven's sake.

Do you really love this,
does it make your soul brave?
If the answer is no,
aren't you simply a slave?

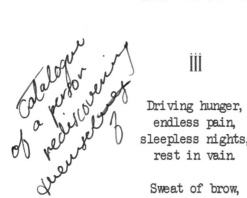

about a few schemed poems, most of the poems in this piece are short + free verse

STRENGTH

COURAGE/ COMPASSION/ SELF-CONFIDENCE

STRENGTH

unlikely courage

i

I am not strong

           like a blast

      but like silent stone

    beneath the froth of great falls.

STRENGTH

ii

What an honour it is,
to know
the remarkable glory of your skin
the holy sanctuary of your embrace.

So lucky am I,
that when all I am is agony,
and my skin screams for silence,
even then,
I still long for your touch.

STRENGTH

iii

Do not fix the vase.

You never needed a container.

But a jagged edge instead.

THE
HERMIT

SELF-REFLECTION /SOLITUDE//SOUL SEARCHING

THE HERMIT

i

Calm as mirror glass,
Smooth as silk.
You would never know.

The tempest behind
this satin smile,

Is raging.

Determined

To swallow

Me whole.

THE HERMIT

ii

More acceptance of femininity

Can you Imagine...
The Loss.
The Crash
The transition from black to red.

The bad men sleeping alone,
The empty make-up bags,
The scent of skin and not perfume.

The wild split ends.
The bare skin as it breathes.
The voices as they rise above the din.

Can you imagine...
If only every woman
accepted herself.
Exactly as she is?

No mask.
No lacquer
No shine.
No shame.

What a beautiful world that would be.

THE HERMIT

iii

There can be no better company,
than the steady crackling fires
of one's own soul,
the calm song of one's own breath,
and the utter acceptance of one's own heart.

THE
WHEEL OF FORTUNE

CHANGE/FATE/LUCK

WHEEL OF FORTUNE

i

Oh, Precious Heart,
beating slower
with every tick
of the needle.

Kneel before the wheel *of change?*
and spin,
praying
for health.

This turn,
it could be you.

With cracking skin,
Under scratchy starch sheets,
beneath high vaulted church ceilings
and sterile light.

My religion is chance,
my hell,
dark bloody walls
and a throat full of razor blades,
burning eternally with fever
for sin I do not remember.

To: suicide? attempt

I will pray then,
for better luck next time,
and hope,
that one day
I too

43

will wear the invisible crown.

WHEEL OF FORTUNE

ii

Cool peppermint and wintergreen.
A crust of ice cracks.

Cinnamon spice,
yuletide embers.

Gingersnaps that crumble.
A mulled rich red,
crisp arctic white.

I swallow them down
both chill and warm,

For what is cosy
without the cold?

The world stills.
Festive lights a haze.

winter is on my tongue,
but you are on my mind.

WHEEL OF FORTUNE

iii

The ice
crisp,
and sharp,
cracks.

An eggshell.
From which tendrils of lush promise,
will crown and breathe.

Born again,
with roots that roam the chill beneath.

Searching
for the end of winter,
for sunlight,
and warmth
long forgotten.

birth!
the end
of winter
rebirth

46

JUSTICE

BALANCE/ CLARITY/ DIGNITY

JUSTICE

i

Petals too open.
Grainy, imperfect.

Ivory silk-stained gold by the dawn.

Do not pluck her, rip her from the dirt.
for enchanted she is not.

The glass dome,
foreign,
is torture,
as is perfection.

Do not shroud her in decadent perfume,
instead inhale the rain-soaked earth.

Or prick your thumb upon her thorns,
and bleed.

For her raw mortality,
the price is high,
the prize incandescent,
but only for those who stop to smell the roses.

JUSTICE

ii

Hear my laugh in turning pages,
That twinkle in dotted eyes.
My wisdom in scribbled margin notes,
my voice still the ignoblest of metres.

See my courage in the swirling font,
my smile in calligraphy curved.
My soul is here phonetically,
Locked in ink,
the key imaginary.

I am pressed between the paragraphs,
a phantom of indents and space.
So now you might remember me,
in black and white.

Hold me in your hands and know,
the truth of my memory is yours to keep,
whether you like it or not.

JUSTICE

iii

Firebird, caged.
Staring beyond glassy almond windows.
Encased in broken bone and failing flesh,
electrified.

There is no escape.

Yet still, you hover, ablaze,
Your phoenix call echoing in the ink
of this unspoken sorrow.

THE
HANGED MAN

LETTING GO/ UNCERTAINTY/ CONFINEMENT

THE HANGED MAN

I

She did not love men.
She loved women.

Healing them,
Holding their labouring hands,
And wiping their sweat-slick brows.
Cooling their fevers,
Taming their cramps,
Hand stitching their broken hearts.

She too,
revered the earth,
for giving her the tools,
to heal,
this way.

Herbs,
Crystals,
Flowers,
Fruit.

Feminine power,
lain in the shadowy crucible
beneath the pestle of her inheritance.

Made potent by the
wisdom of her mother's mother
Passed from wrinkled palm to
childish eyes wide with wonder.

Slowly ground with power forged
by the very oppression
that had formed them

She did not love men,
So, when they came for her,
and made her stand upon the gallows,
caressing her silken neck
with brazen rope.

Tongues tempting her fury with that word.

Witch

She cried to see the women she loved
do nothing
in the face of
such violation
of her virgin skin.

It was not the love bite of the noose,
nor the way that gravity held her
in her final moments.

Male arms terrifying,
too strong,
robbing her breath
before snapping her spine.

It was the eyes of women
the ones she loved most,
that drained her dry.

Watching her magic
spilled like blood.

Standing there.

Stone still.

Her craft made worthless,
as she dangled in silence
so thick
it could choke.

The men watched on,
content they had tamed her
and her sisters as well.

THE HANGED MAN

ii

It's just a phase
You're going through.

You said.

So, I waned...

Drifting from the path
Burying myself in reality.

But then the waxing came,
Unstoppable as a storm
Drinking in the pine rich air,
and bathing in buttered light.

My magic stirs.

Turns out,
The phase was never magic.

It was you.

THE HANGED MAN

iii

Be yourself.
Ha.
No.
Slip it on.
Like lingerie,
or armour.

Their wish is our command.

Slut.
Prude.
Shorty.
Giraffe.
Emotional.
Heartless.
Workaholic.
Unambitious.
Fatty.
Anorexic.
Daughter.
Slob.
Clean-Freak.
Tomboy.
Princess.
Wife.
Mistress.
Seductress.
Fake.

Real.
Cougar.
Cock tease.
Dom
Sub.
Damsel.
Dragon.

Which mask did you slip on this morning?

And...

Will you wear it with pride?

Overall: discovering and rediscovering by unearthing precious femininity

DEATH

ENDINGS/ LOSS/ RESOLUTION

DEATH

i

Petrichor floods my lungs,
Cement dust coats my tongue.
Bare soles which slapped warm stone
Rocking on this porch now, alone.

Here I sit, basking.

Misted by the golden twilight
Of my waning solar wisdom

And sodden
With waxing lunar sadness.

DEATH

ii

It stares at you,
inky black voids of infinity.

Will it buck or snicker?

Do not wait to discover.

Bridle the beast.
And gallop,
valiant,
into the dying of the light.

DEATH

iii

And while my prose was like a knife,
killing you slowly
slice by slice

My poetry was a bullet
straight to the heart.

TEMPERANCE

MODESTY/ HEALING/ CONTROL

TEMPERANCE

i

She runs,
wild.

Fantasy dressed in a dream

Skirt billowing, a cloud,
Snagged by a single thorn.

Doubt,
sheer and sharp,
tears the flat silken grain asunder.

An anxious bloody cancer.
A Sanguine Bloom
It grows.

Tainting this ecrus hope a cautious crimson

TEMPERANCE

ii

Tenderness.

The act of watching
Day by day
Hour by hour
Motionless
With the agony of anticipation
Waiting with undying loyalty
For a flower to bloom
Instead of plucking another
Already open.

TEMPERANCE

iii

And if I knew
my cocoon
would form of
jagged knives,
broken glass,
and endless nights
of untold agony...

Would I have welcomed it
to spread these wings?

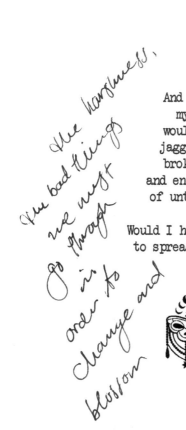

the harshness, the bad things we must go through in order to change and blossom

THE
DEVIL

WRATH/DESTRUCTION/DEPRESSION

THE DEVIL

i

I cast my spell,
a thousand wicks.
Flickering, wild
and bright
and quick.

My shadow's here,
across the wall.
Dark and clear,
and long and tall.

shadow work

I greet her once,
I shake her hand
and promise her,
she'll not be damned.

I want to know her,
walk side by side.
To learn my darkness,
and forgo my pride.

THE DEVIL

ii

I stand in a tent of horrors.

The cruellest girl
staring out at me
everywhere
and nowhere
merciless eyes burning my skin
branding me.

Failure.
Fake.
Fraud.

She sneers.

Ugly.
Weak.
Pathetic.

She vows.

I flee.
Stumbling from the house of mirrors.

•)●(•·•·+

THE DEVIL

iii

Sometimes
in all my pain,
I am so very tempted
to give up.

Sometimes
there is wrath in this flesh,
Nerves firing,
driving me to gentle madness.

Sometimes
I feel the sloth in my bones
like quicksand,
beckoning.

Sometimes
Fog rolls through my mind
an opiate kick
of tantalising nothingness.

They lull me,
promising sweet oblivion,
or long-sought justice,
against this failing shell,
Release from this torment.

And yet,

because of so many,
I fight the devil's lure.

I say,
Not today.

I have mermaids to swim with,
unicorns to ride.
dragons to fly,
magic to make.

Most importantly though,
I have stories to tell,
and my saviours,
the people willing to listen

THE
TOWER

AWAKENING/ CALAMITY/ DANGER

THE TOWER

i

High above the clouds,
I gaze upon my life.

Above the fog of indoctrination
The pollution of opinion
The poison of judgement.

I see the truth.

I am so exceedingly small.
The world so very wide.

And so,

I breathe a little easier.

discovery and rediscovery of the self through hardship & resilience

THE TOWER

ii

I built walls so very high,
not to keep others out,
nor to shut my heart away.

I built walls so very high,
to discover,
who would learn to climb

73

THE TOWER

iii

How pleasant it must be,
to view the world
through the stained-glass
of your gilded tower.

How privileged you are
to close the door on reality
whilst sucking a silver spoon
laden with impunity.

THE
STAR

INSPIRATION/FAITH/TRANQUILITY

THE STAR

i

I am a shooting star,
   Orbiting words.

Caught in the gravity
   of pages turned.

THE STAR

ii

Pitter pat,
hot rain on tin roofs sizzle.

Plink plonk

Chill droplets roll from ceramic gutters.

Gaia's drumming up the sounds of war,
Or is this her grief battering the panes?

The pelting fists of fluid frost,
or,
one dare hope,
the thrumming torrent of joyous salt,
perhaps?

THE STAR

The sky of other blanket of the ground

iii

Starry starry night,
Whorls of colour and of light.
A canvas blanketing this world,
Of pain and love, emotion swirled.

THE
MOON

ANGUISH/ INSTABILITY/ ILLUSION

THE MOON

i

Blood slicked thighs,
her ragged pulse pulls her
glowing milky face skyward.

She sees the moon,
in its darkest phase,
feels its gravity tugging her shedding skin
as she too is led by its thrall.

Leaning back on her haunches,
spine arched
like a waxing lunar crescent,
she howls.

Deep,
sobering,
a song to her sister.

She too knows what pain it is,
to live a life of cycles,
her soul captive and helpless
to the phases of darkness and light.

THE MOON

ii

Antlers buried against her skull,
the urban sprawl,
is far too dull,
for a creature of such potent power,
a child born of the witching hour.

She stalks the forest
a naked Queen,
amongst her subjects,
the lushest green.

The branches tangle in her hair,
for she belongs to the forest,
the earth,
the air.

She's bathed in some cold stag's warm blood.
an act of faith, an act of love.

For the forest it just gives and takes,
the life within an endless ache.
Still, she walks amongst the chaos, the pain,
Welcoming the thunder, revering the rain.

THE MOON

iii

I see her.
The girl I was.
The enigma I am
The wise woman I want to become.
Each phase silhouetted
by the shadow
of my despair,
and against the abyss
of my pain.
I embrace the dark side of my soul.
For without it
I will never grow full
and shine.

THE
SUN

CONFIDENCE/HARMONY/SOULMATES

SUN

i

The sky is on fire.

Clementine,
carmine,
crimson,
and cherry.

My black mirror calls.

After all,
I have the perfect filter for this.

SUN

ii

Buttery sunbeams fall,
tendrils of Eros's beard.

Butterflies scat through motion
In long daylight hours that
creep like hungry fingers,
reaching for the night.

The moon watches on,
her gaze adoring.
Eclipsed by his summer evening,
But seductive all the same.

Soon though,
he will diminish once more.

Just to see her shine.

SUN

iii

Hey there, Wildflower.
Swaying in the sun.
Does it make you sad to know
you'll die when summer's done?

No.

For Spring will come again.
I only must reach up to the sun,
and faithfully open.

86

JUDGEMENT

RENEWAL/ COMPOSURE/ EVOLUTION

JUDGEMENT

I

To judge you is to admit my shame.
To announce everything
that is wrong with me.

When I judge you,
I paint it
in bright red upon your skin
For all the world to see.

JUDGEMENT

ii

Who am I to slam the gavel
and sentence
When I have not attended the trial?

Who am I to judge?

JUDGEMENT

iii

It's in my blood,
it's in my stare.

Look at those shoes,
check out that hair.

Though years may pass
and age may daunt

I'm still that girl
they loved to taunt.

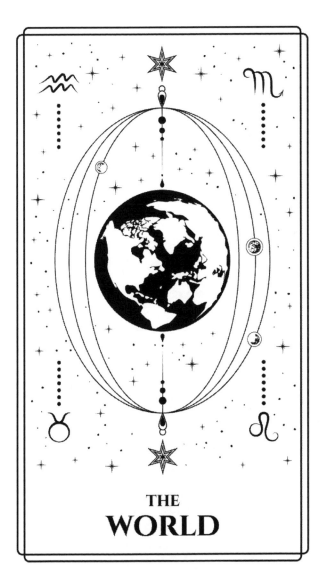

THE
WORLD

WHOLENESS/PEACE/FULFILMENT

WORLD

i

She was beautiful,
once.

But sublimity was lost
Self-importance
growing larger as she shrank

We drew
permanent cityscapes
onto her face,
obscuring her unwelcome familiarity.

Tattooed flawless flesh
instead with roads,
so we might escape the
banality of her curves.

We filled her sagging skin,
with mounds of gaudy plastic
for our pleasures.

Pumping her lungs full of smoke,
so that we might keep her manageable.

With each chemical ring,
each fossil plume,
she chokes.

An aesthetic act,

that thins the blood of estuaries ancient,
polluting those once plump lips
we must still kiss.

She is remade smooth and malleable,
barren,
painted,
and augmented.

She asks,
body growing feverish each passing year:

Why can you not just let me be wild?

We answer:
For fear that you,
as most women,
will be far too much to handle.

WORLD

ii

This Chartreuse dream,
it plagues me.

Starting at my stem,
creeping like vines,
mossy and lush,
jading my grey matter.

Sending lime sparks between synapses.
Taking root in the emerald,
kelpie tangle of medulla flesh.

It is a seed, floating,
A lily-pad in my malachite meninges, thin.
An olive fruit that quenches my thirst
With minty juices,
A flowering, viridian forest tongue.

A word so very viridescent.

WORLD

iii

Such devastation
shall befall me,
holding the power
to create worlds
in the palms of my hands.

What exquisite agony it is
to know
that this world
will never be enough.

ABOUT THE AUTHOR

28-year-old British writer Kristy Nicolle is achieving freedom from the pain of her Ehlers Danlos Syndrome diagnosis by bringing fantasy worlds to life for her readers. Kristy enjoys spending time in her fuzzy PJs with her kitty arch nemesis, Moo, and loves all things mermaids, unicorns, and glitter!

Award-winning author of over a million published words, Kristy Nicolle is currently working on a supersized series called The Kristy Nicolle Fantasy Infiniverse.

I Am Arcana is Kristy Nicolle's debut poetry collection.

Keep up to date with Kristy Nicolle @

www.kristynicolle.com

Fantasy Romance Titles By Kristy Nicolle

The Queens of Fantasy Saga

Trilogy One- The Tidal Kiss Trilogy (Mermaids)

The Kiss That Killed Me

The Kiss That Saved Me

The Kiss That Changed me

Tidal Kiss Short Stories

Waiting For Gideon

Beyond The Shallows

Tidal Kiss Novellas

Vexed

Trilogy Two- The Ashen Touch Trilogy (Demons and The Underworld)

The Opal Blade

The Onyx Hourglass

The Obsidian Shard

Ashen Touch Short Stories

A Touch of Smoke And Snow

DYSTOPIAN ROMANCE TITLES BY KRISTY NICOLLE

(Arranged Blind Marriage By Science)
Something Blue- A Standalone Dystopian Romance Novel

ACKNOWLEDGEMENTS

A huge thank you to all my incredible readers, who have always truly supported me, whether I'm writing poetry or fiction. I'm so grateful to my family, my incredible partner Mark, my editor, my fabulous PA Jenna Martinez, and in particular, Leeah Minick, who saw the poet in me when I could not and pushed me to publish this collection.

I hope you've loved this poetic journey through the world of Tarot!

Stay magical x